Take a journey over the next 52 weeks to discover the Hidden Truth of your identity as God's Beloved Daughter.

Ashley Nute Weston is the owner and designer of Hidden Truth Jewelry, a handmade jewelry line inspired by the Lord to encourage women and girls in the faith with scripture hidden on the back of each piece. She is a women's ministry speaker and a passionate lover of the Word of God.

Cherrie Nute Farley is a professional and award winning artist, who has created artwork for SC Governor Carol Campbell as well as President Ronald Reagan. She is a women's ministry speaker and has worked as a short term missionary to Nicaragua over the last 20 years.

PUBLISHED BY HIDDEN TRUTH JEWELRY

Cherrie Nute Farley (left) and Ashley Nute Weston (right)

I AM
WHO YOU SAY
I AM

Weekly Devotions for Women

Ashley Nute Weston

Artwork by Cherrie Nute Farley

Hidden Truth Jewelry

P.O. Box 6984

Columbia, SC 29206

www.HiddenTruthJewelry.com

Ordering Information:

For details, contact ashley@hiddentruthjewelry.com

For inquiries on purchasing original artwork, contact cherrienuteart@aol.com

Printed in the United States of America on SFI Certified paper.

First Edition

ISBN: 978-1-09834-299-9

TABLE OF CONTENTS

FOREWARD

I Am Who You Say I Am is a wonderfully written book that speaks to the women of the world, and explains to them how God can be present in their lives, in every single moment. The author uses a unique and effective method to present the material. Each section begins with a bible verse, is then followed by a short narrative that relays a related personal experience from the author. The author then writes directly to the reader, and finishes with a personal prayer.

The strength of this manuscript is both its unique and useful method for delivering the author's message, as well as the clear passion and emotion the author has for this topic. The author manages to convey a strong sense of God, the belief that anyone can feel God's presence in every moment of their lives, and the steps needed to achieve this goal. The author does all of this without seeming as if she is lecturing or dictating specific actions to the reader. The reader feels engaged in the topic and comforted by the discussion, rather than feeling as if someone who has this knowledge is telling her what to do in a manner that is condescending or pushy.

I Am Who You Say I Am is a beautifully written, well-organized, and informative book that is sure to engage any reader from the first page. The author does a wonderful job relaying her thoughts in a way that is enjoyable for all readers.

HEY BELOVED DAUGHTER OF GOD!

Within the pages of this book is an invitation. Your amazing Heavenly Father wants to open the door to His truths about who you are to Him, who He created you to be, and your truest identity in His Beloved Son, Jesus Christ. Over the next fifty-two weeks, you are invited to go on an adventure with Daddy God!! Each week, as you meditate on one of the scriptures revealing your identity, listen attentively for the loving whispers of His Holy Spirit within you. It's the same Spirit that raised Christ from the dead. As you allow the truth of who He says you are into your thoughts, He will raise dead things in your heart to life and you will experience true JOY! Jesus Christ is the way, the truth, and the life. He is the door to this incredible journey!

Before you begin, ask yourself these questions—"Is Jesus Christ my Lord and Savior?" "Have I truly surrendered all to him?" If so, great! Forge on ahead, sweet sister! If not, simply ask him now, *"Dear Jesus, I want you to be Lord of everything in my life. I recognize I am a sinner in need of a Savior. Please forgive me and wash me clean in your precious blood. You are the perfect sacrifice. I receive you now and your gift of salvation! I now walk through you, the door of salvation!*

Let the journey begin!

MORE PRECIOUS THAN JEWELS

"She is far more precious than jewels."

Proverbs 31:10b ESV

The day my husband whisked me off my feet and asked me to be his wife forever with a beautiful diamond engagement ring was one of the best days of my life. He planned for that moment, prepared for it, saved money for it, and chose just the perfect symbol of his love to give to me. Every little girl thinks about this moment–the long awaited knight in shining armor with his priceless sign of the covenant of love he has chosen to make with his beloved. The engagement ring is a cherished gift to a bride-to-be as it is a sign that she is cherished and even more precious than jewels to him.

Beloved Daughter of God, Father God cherishes you. You are, to Him, far more precious than jewels. You are to Him more beautiful than the most magnificent flowers of the field! As a sign of Father's great love for you, He sent His one and only Son, Jesus Christ, to be yours forever. Jesus has given you His Holy Spirit as a sign of his covenant love for you—a priceless reminder that just like in a marriage, he will never leave you, always care for you, provide for you, and love you unconditionally. He is yours and you are His forever. Just as a beloved wife looks down upon the beautiful diamond ring on her finger to remember her husband's love, or as master gardener looks proudly at the abundant springtime blooms his hands labored over, listen closely for the Holy Spirit's whispers of loving reminders of his presence, provision, guidance, and protection. God loves you, beloved daughter of God, and your truest identity is more precious than jewels to Him.

Prayer: Dear Heavenly Father, thank you for cherishing me more than the rarest of gemstones! What a beautiful assurance to know I am loved so much by the Creator of the universe! I reject any other labels that this world has tried to place on me and receive only your identity for me as more precious than jewels! In Jesus' name, Amen!

CHILD OF GOD

"See what great love the Father has lavished on us, that we should be called children of God! And that is what we are!"

1 John 3:1 NIV

The first time my husband and I held our long awaited first born child, Elizabeth Grace, we fell in love with her. As I watched my husband, who had become a dad in a moment's time, hold her, I watched how he gazed upon her with pure joy. I could see him excitedly scan her whole life for all the wonderful memories they would have—how he wanted to show her his love, play with her, teach her, and protect her. He loved her in an instant as much as one human could, even though this tiny little bundle did not yet even understand what the meaning of love was, nor was capable of even loving back.

Beloved Daughter of God, Father God, is calling all of His daughters back to Him. He wants to replace any ashes experienced in this world that may have created a tainted relationship with Him to one of pure beauty. In the protective loving arms of Father, Son, and Holy Spirit, He wants to clothe you in purple robes of righteousness. He wants you to feel the shelter and strength of His protective embrace. He doesn't want you to worry about tomorrow but trust that He will provide everything you need. When did we as daughters of God grow up and doubt God's love for us? When did we start questioning that God might leave us, not provide for us, protect us, or He would let us down? What did God do to lose our trust? Was it truly God that lost our trust, or did we misunderstand his ways and miss His whispers of love? Beloved daughter of God, when your Heavenly Father gazes upon you, He is looking at you with eyes and a heart of pure love. Infinitely more times than when we as parents meet our babies for the first-time. Receive His love today and your position as Child of God. This is your truest identity, God's beloved daughter.

Prayer: Dear Heavenly Father, thank you for adopting me into your royal family! What an honor and privilege to be called your child. With this mindset, I will live my life in confident assurance that my daddy in Heaven will always love me, protect me, and provide for me. I love you! In Jesus' name, Amen!

MADE IN GOD'S IMAGE

"Then God said, "Let us make human beings in our image, to be like us. They will reign over the fish in the sea, the birds in the sky, the livestock, all the wild animals on the earth, and the small animals that scurry along the ground."

GENESIS 1:26 NLT

When my daughter turned 6 years old, all she wanted was the ever so popular American Girl Doll. With much anticipation of which doll to choose, our family traveled to the store in celebration of her birthday. Much to my surprise, you could actually "create" your own doll to look just like you. You could choose every little detail from skin, hair, and eye color to distinguishing details like freckles, face shape, and even personality! What fun it was for my daughter to create a unique one-of-a-kind doll in her image to represent her!

Beloved Daughter of God, on the sixth day of creation, God purposefully and lovingly thought about you. Yes, after creating the most glorious place for you to live, with all the resources you would need to thrive in this world, God had a plan to create you in His image. In this privileged plan, you were purposed to rule and reign over all His creation. This plan was again restored after the redeemed work Jesus did on the cross. In John 14:12, Jesus said that anyone who has faith in him will do what he did, and when Jesus returned to Heaven, he sent his Holy Spirit to help us accomplish and walk in this powerful promise. You were made in His image and through faith in Christ, you are a part of Christ's body, fully equipped to walk out this destiny day after day just as Jesus did. You get to partner with God in Christ through the Holy Spirit to fulfill His original purpose to overcome the flesh, to rule and reign in this earth, to have dominion and subdue it, and to live as Jesus did fueled by His sacrificial love, a love that casts out all fear and never fails. So, receive this calling and boldly walk out your truest identity now and forever as His Beloved Daughter, made in God's Image.

Prayer: Thank you Heavenly Father, Lord Jesus, and Holy Spirit that I have been made powerfully, purposefully, and lovingly in Your image. I boldly receive this identity and will walk confidently knowing I have been empowered because I was made in your image!

VICTORIOUS

"If God is for us, who can be against us?"

Romans 8:31 NIV

Many years ago, I had a very powerful dream, that the Lord used to teach, encourage, and train me. There was a great battle taking place between a loved one and the enemy. This loved one was unarmed for the battle, but God placed me in the middle of the battle laying down on the ground with Jesus on one side of me and God the Father on the other. As the battle raged, I would pray bold prayers looking up toward Heaven. A grand display of fireworks filled the sky as prayers were spoken and claimed. My loved one, although unarmed, dodged all the bullets and the enemy defeated himself!

Beloved Daughter of God, if your Heavenly Father is for you, who then can be against you? Father God wants you to know today that in Him, you are victorious! Do not be afraid if you find yourself in the middle of a raging war. Do not be overcome with fear if you feel an enemy attack and fiery bullets being shot at you. Don't for one second give up hope or get discouraged. You are equipped in every way to be victorious in each single battle. You are not alone, but you are surrounded on every side by God the Father, God the Son, and God the Holy Spirit. The weapons you have been given are not weapons of this world, but spiritual weapons. He has also given you brothers and sisters in Christ to help support you along the way. You are a part of His church, the bride of Christ, and he will never leave you nor forsake you! Unwavering faith, confident intentional prayers, linked arms with fellow believers, courage and unshakable trust in the One who defeated the cross and death, Jesus Christ, is how you will see the enemy defeated.

Remember, God IS for you, and He has given you the perfect spiritual tools to partner with the armies of Heaven to be victorious. This is your truest identity, beloved Daughter of God– VICTORIOUS in Christ!

Prayer: Dear Father, Son and Holy Spirit, in you I declare that I am victorious! I will not fear what my eyes can see or my heart feels but will trust your promises that nothing is impossible with you! I am victorious because I remain secure in the One who is victorious over all things! In Jesus' name, Amen!

NEW CREATION

"Therefore, if anyone is in Christ, the new creation has come: The old has gone, the new is here!"

2 CORINTHIANS 5:17

Last summer, my family and I took a sun filled vacation to our beloved South Carolina Coastline, Litchfield Beach. One morning during our stay, the Lord woke me up early and I could not go back to sleep. I decided I would go sit out and worship Him on the balcony overlooking the ocean and enjoy the beautiful creation He had created. As night turned to day and the magnificent light of dawn broke through the clouds, I sat in awe of God's marvelous new creation that each day brings. Passionate deep pinks and gorgeous steaks of purple filled the sky as the day was awakening from the dark of night.

Beloved Daughter of God, more beautiful than any break of dawn or sunset that fills the sky are you to your Heavenly Father. Just as God begins each day as a new creation in the rhythms of nature, He created you into a new creation when you gave your life to Jesus Christ as Lord and Savior. Even though nothing physically might have changed, spiritually you became brand new. Once distant and broken in relationship to God, now with Christ's shed blood covering all your sins and God's Holy Spirit inside of you, you are joined to your Father's heart forever. The dark of night in your old sinful nature is now gone and the newness of His Spirit inside of you is at work, powerfully and wonderfully! You are new and forever changed in a glorious way! This is your truest identity, Daughter of God—a New Creation!

Prayer: Thank you Jesus for being my Lord and Savior. In you, I have been made new! I declare my old self has gone and my new self in Christ is here! Help me remain in you daily and walk boldly in the freedom you died to give me now and forever! In Jesus' mighty name, Amen!

NEVER AGAIN SEPARATED FROM GOD'S LOVE

"Nothing in all creation will ever be able to separate us from the love of God that is revealed in Christ Jesus our Lord."

ROMANS 8:39B NLT

Growing up as a child, there were so many things I needed help with from my parents. What I needed, but could not get on my own, my parents provided. I had to completely rely on them to generously provide me with food, clothing, shelter, transportation, education, community, love, and much more. Now, years later as a parent myself, this great need children have comes full circle as it is my great honor and privilege to give my kids what they cannot obtain themselves.

Beloved Daughter of God, from the beginning of time, God had a great plan to provide you with the abundant eternal life of experiencing His glorious loving presence all the time. However, we as humans became separated from Him when sin entered this world through the disobedience of Adam and Eve. Our relationship with our loving Heavenly Father had to be continually restored through the covenant of animal sacrifice. God had a greater plan and sent His perfect Son, Jesus Christ, to rescue you and provide an eternal gift of salvation because you could not obtain this alone. You no longer have to worry if you are good enough or have followed enough rules, because you were bought by the precious blood of Jesus. Salvation comes by faith alone, not works. You have been adopted as a child of God, and once you receive His gift of love by grace through faith, it is an irrevocable covenant. Your old self and sinful nature have passed away and you have become brand new. The law and its righteous requirements were fully met in us with what Jesus accomplished in his life, death, and resurrection. What you could not obtain yourself, God has provided. With this truth comes a promise. He will continue to supply you with everything you need in Him. This truth is your truest identity, Beloved Daughter of God—never again separated from God's love.

Prayer: Jesus, my Lord and Savior, thank you for doing for me what I could not do! Thank you for restoring my relationship with Father God and the wonderful gift of eternal salvation, security, and love. I shall never fear again for I know that I will always be with you. Amen.

FEARFULLY AND WONDERFULLY MADE

"I praise you because I am fearfully and wonderfully made; your works are wonderful,
I know that full well."

PSALM 139:14 NIV

A huge turning point in my life happened the summer before my sixth grade year. All the girls I knew greatly anticipated middle school cheerleading tryouts. Yes, anyone who was anyone wanted to be a cheerleader. Naturally, when the big day came, this quirky adolescent girl gave it her best shot to be in the highly sought after "club" of girls. Days later, after finding out I didn't make the cut to be a cheerleader, I was devastated. My talents and skills were different than all the other girls, because God had other plans just for me.

Beloved Daughter of God, the world wants to make you think that you are not special. The world wants to point out the things of which that you are not good. The world may send you a message that you are not enough or are a failure at certain things. The truth is that God made you, and EVERYTHING God made is good. His ways are not our ways, His thoughts are higher than ours. God planned everything about you even down to how many hairs you have on your head, and He declared that it was good. Do not for one moment think you are not beautiful to Him. When your Heavenly Daddy looks at you, He is well pleased at the wonderful creation He has made. Open your eyes to see that everything about you that is unique and for an extraordinary purpose. There is beauty in the YOU that He made for you to be. Rocks by themselves may not appear to be beautiful, but when mixed with rushing water, they become one of the most beautiful things in creation—a waterfall! When you allow God to shape you into the wonderful creation He intended for you to become, all of creation takes notice! Press into the One who created you and see that you are fearfully and wonderfully made because you are not like all the rest of His daughters. You are uniquely you! This is your truest identity—fearfully and wonderfully created by God.

Prayer: Thank you Heavenly Father for creating me just as I am. Forgive me for not liking completely who I am because of what the world says is desirable. I have been created in every way perfect in your eyes for the very specific purpose in which you created me for. My personality, physical features, abilities, likes and dislikes, and giftings all work together on purpose. I will not compare myself to others, but walk confidently knowing I was made a masterpiece by my loving Master! In Jesus' name, Amen!

GIVEN ACCESS TO THE THRONE

"Let us then approach God's throne of grace with confidence, so that we may receive mercy and find grace to help us in our time of need."

HEBREWS 4:16 NIV

At the break of dawn, or the when the sun begins to set, when powerful beams of brilliant colored light fills the sky, the earth becomes crowned with the majesty of our Sovereign God Almighty. Throughout the day, when I look up at the sky, and see the bright sun, the beautiful clouds and all that is above, I am reminded how big God is and how small I am. God is so big, our human minds cannot even fathom it. He is Creator of all, more powerful than any other force in existence, and deserves nothing short of our highest praises.

Beloved Daughter of God, there is good news for you! You have been given complete access to the throne of God through the shed blood of Jesus Christ. Yes, you can boldly and confidently approach God's mighty and powerful throne knowing you will be met with mercy, love, and grace every time! Can you imagine approaching the President of the United States anytime with the confidence of having his undivided attention and immediate help? Your Heavenly Father has given you even greater assurance that you have complete access to Him anytime. He not only hears you, but is also gladly willing to help you immediately! As you come to His throne of grace, you are met with love, peace, joy, hope, and every good thing that your amazing Daddy has to offer! Just look up and as you see His magnificent creation in the sky, Your Father is above it all! Hallelujah! GO, Daughter of God, now and often, to Father God's Throne with confidence because you have been given permanent access to it! For this is your truest identity as a Beloved Daughter of God.

Prayer: Dear Heavenly Father, Wow. I am so humbled and honored that you, as Creator of the entire world, always have time to listen to me, help me, and love me. My heart feels safe and secure knowing that I can always come to talk and spend time with you at any moment in time! What a blessed assurance that can never be taken away from me! In Jesus' Holy name, Amen!

PURPOSED BY GOD

"For I know the plans I have for you," declares the Lord, "plans to prosper
you and not to harm you, plans to give you hope and a future."

JEREMIAH 29:11 NIV

Do you like a plan? Are you a goal setter? Do you like to know the schedule so you can seize the day, conquer the territory ahead, and know the rules to win? When I trained for my first marathon, I followed a well thought out plan set in place by expert and seasoned runners. The plan suggested daily training runs, meal plans, rest plans, and strength training every day for four months leading up to the race. The experts knew the method to achieving the set goal of running a long 26.2 miles, because they had run the race before. After following their wisdom and set plan, four months later, strong from persevering endurance, I accomplished the race successfully.

Beloved Daughter of God, since the beginning of time, your Heavenly Father has had a plan. In that plan, He thought about you. He created a beautiful Earth for you to enjoy and gave you His people to be in community with those who are His body. The only way you can know what this good plan is for your life, is to seek Him. He may not reveal the entire plan, as His ways are higher than yours and thoughts are far better than what you can imagine. Trust Him that as you submit yourself to His good plan, you will find the amazing purpose He created you for, one that will fulfill every desire you have deep in your heart. If you find yourself in a season that is difficult, just know it's just part of the plan, and God promises to work everything out in His plan for good as you look to Him. He has a plan and a great purpose for your life. Enjoy the journey with Him to discover it! For this is your truest identity as a beloved Daughter of God—*Purposed by God.*

Prayer: What a comfort to know that you have a good plan for me, Heavenly Father! Even if the
plan looks blurry or different than what I hoped at times, I will ever the more trust in you because I
know that you are good, and you love me! In Jesus' name, Amen.

UNSTOPPABLE WITH HIS HELP

"The LORD is my rock, my fortress, and my savior; my God is my rock, in whom I find protection. He is my shield, the power that saves me, and my place of safety.

PSALM 18:2 NLT

Have you ever felt unstoppable before? Maybe it was on your high school or college graduation day, when you had completed such a great achievement with endless opportunities ahead ready for you to conquer? Perhaps it was when you completed a hard task in which you persevered didn't give up? Maybe it was just on a normal day, after a couple cups of coffee, fired up and ready to take on anything ahead!?

Beloved Daughter of God, when you are in your Father's tender care, no mountain, no valley, no unchartered path can stop you. Nothing can stop you! This glorious truth is your identity that He has bestowed upon you to help you walk boldly, run fearlessly, believe impossibilities, and overcome all odds! Yes, no matter what stands in your way, when you let God lead you, together anything is possible. If you wake up and feel weak, press into Him and He will strengthen you. When you don't know what to do, God is a whisper away to wisely council you on His way. When fear wants to taunt you into lots of "what if" scenarios, God's loving presence will destroy those nasty lies of the enemy as you draw near to Him. Shift any perspective the world has persuaded you to believe, or your past has deceived you into believing will be the pattern, to God's perspective of possibilities. The Bible says in Mark 11:23, "If anyone says to this mountain, Go throw yourself into the sea, and does not doubt in their heart but believes that what he says will happen." Believe dear daughter that God can do immeasurably more than all you ask or imagine according to His good purposes. Stand close to Him at all times and find this identity to be your constant reality, for this is your truest identity as a beloved Daughter of God—*Unstoppable with His Help!*

Prayer: Lord, forgive me for believing lies that I cannot do hard things. Forgive me for doubting you. I now put on for once and all your identity for me, Unstoppable with Your Help! In Jesus' mighty name, Amen!

CONFIDENT IN GOOD WORK

"And I am sure of this, that he who began a good work in you will bring it to completion at the day of Jesus Christ."

Philippians 1:6 ESV

Many years ago, I set out a lofty goal of running a marathon. Knowing I would need support as well as wanting to run with a purpose, I joined the local "Team in Training" put on by the Leukemia & Lymphoma Society. Putting my eyes on the prize of completing 26.2 long miles along with raising money in honor of my late grandfather who passed away from the disease, I met my goal alongside my teammates I had trained with the previous five months. We made the decision to run the race, eyes on the goal, and together we were confident we could stay the course and win the prize!

Beloved Daughter of God, did you know that you can be absolutely confident in the good work God began in you when you trusted Jesus as Lord and Savior? Many people have said the Christian faith is like running a marathon, having highs and lows, but with your eye on the end goal you will see the prize of your faith….His peace, joy, hope, strength, love and salvation.

Sometimes life seems like an uphill climb, but God will always give you confidence in His promises that He will use all things for good as you keep your eyes on Him and follow in humble obedience. Even when the journey is difficult, as you press into Him, you will see the sweet gifts of mercy and grace planted like fragrant flowers along the path. Don't ever give up hope even if you feel like God has prolonged answering a deep desire. Spending time with Him and experiencing His comforting and strengthening presence is truly the most glorious gift. He will give you His perspective as you journey this path with Him and give you a peace that you can trust where He leads. God will work all things out for good for you because you love Him, according to His good purposes. In this dear daughter, you can be confident! For this is your truest identity and promise as a beloved Daughter of God—*Confident in Good Work.*

Prayer: Dear Heavenly Father, thank you that my confidence doesn't lie in what I can see, but in the truth that I believe. Your Word is a promise to me and I boldly declare my identity right now that I am confident in Your Good Work. In Jesus' name, Amen.

CREATED FOR ABUNDANCE

"Now to him who is able to do immeasurably more than all we ask or imagine, according to his power that is at work within us."

Ephesians 3:20 NIV

A few years ago, I tried to plant a vegetable garden. Grand plans were made in my head and visions of an abundance of vegetables to eat filled my mind. I went to the local store to buy all the seeds and plants, and got to work creating the space and planting the plants. However, I got distracted and forgot to water, fertilize, and tend to this little garden enough times that it did not produce what I had envisioned in my head. Summer plans and out of town vacations caused me to neglect this growing garden, and unfortunately the weeds and insects got the best of my vegetable garden. The garden had the potential to yield an abundant harvest of tasty treats, yet in the hands of an unskilled gardener, it turned out far less than that.

Beloved Daughter of God, you were created for abundance. Your life is similar to this envisioned beautiful garden. In the hands of the Master Gardener, your Heavenly Father, you have the potential for immeasurably more than all you can ask or imagine. When you yield your life daily and ultimately to Him, you have the potential to yield a harvest far beyond what you can even dream. In your Daddy's hands, you will be planted, watered, fertilized, and tended to at the perfect time, every time. Your job is to trust Him, choose faith over fear, and pay attention to where He is leading. God's great power will work within you, His chosen vessel, to produce an abundant beautiful harvest! Beloved Daughter, this is your truest identity—created for abundance!

Prayer: Dear Heavenly Father, I yield my life to you completely, now and forever. Grow in me abundant tasty fruit of your Holy Spirit that I may glorify you in every way! How amazing to think that in you, nothing, absolutely nothing, is impossible! In Jesus' name, Amen!

PART OF THE BODY OF CHRIST

"Now you are the body of Christ, and each one of you is a part of it."

1 Corinthians 12:27 NIV

Growing up, my family and I would take a trip to the mountains each summer. It was a highlight of the summer to visit a cooler part of the state, as temperatures can become extremely unbearable in the hot Southern sun. After enjoying a challenging hike, our family would take a break and test our bravery in the frigid mountain stream. Once you got over the initial shock of the drastic temperature change, the dip in the river was surprisingly refreshing. Relaxation would set in as your mind, soul, and body took note of the breathtaking scenery all around and nature itself working together in perfect unity pointing to an awesome God who had created it all.

Beloved Daughter of God, as a follower of Christ, your identity is part of His body. Being a part of the body, God has purposefully created you with unique giftings to use together with fellow believers to fulfill the Great Commission in this world. Yes, you are a vital part of advancing the Gospel and seeing His Kingdom come on earth as it is in heaven. Don't ever look at someone else in comparison feeling less valuable. God created you on purpose with a great purpose in mind and that can only be carried out as you confidently walk in the giftings unique to you. Just as plants, rocks, and vegetation are planted along a stream, they all work together in perfect unity with different functions, not the same. So it is with you, your greatest desires will be fulfilled as you carry out your unique position as the part of the Body you were created to be. This dear daughter is your truest identity, a very special *Part of the Body of Christ."*

Prayer: Thank you, Jesus, that in you, I am a vital part of your body. I will not compare myself with others in feeling less valuable, but will walk confidently in the amazing purpose you created just for me. Show me today, how I can use these special giftings to encourage others.

A SWEET AROMA

"We are a sweet smell of Christ that reaches up to God. It reaches out to those who are being saved from the punishment of sin and to those who are still lost in sin."

2 Corinthians 2:15 NLV

How happy does it make you in the morning to wake up to the smell of a pot of coffee brewing? What emotions are stirred up in your heart when you walk into a kitchen smelling of fresh baked chocolate chip cookies? How does it make you feel to smell fresh laundry? Do you like the smell of freshly cut grass? What about bacon frying in the pan? What a powerful thing the sense of smell is to awaken emotions and draw you to something when that smell is pleasing to the nose!

Beloved Daughter of God, did you know that when you became a new creation in Christ, a sweet and pleasing aroma was lifted up to God from within you? You now carry the aroma of Christ—one of victory, love, peace, joy, hope, faith, and so much more! You are different in the best way, and all of creation takes notice of it! Similar to how your favorite smell draws you closer to it, the sweet smell of Christ that is within you is a blessing wherever you go. Nothing you do can take that away. It is not meant to be hidden, but is a gift meant to be shared with the whole world! Just like the enticing beauty of wildflowers planted along a stream are you, dear daughter, to the world as you bear the smell of victory from Jesus Christ living in you. This sweet smell will draw people in to a hope that can change the world, turn darkness into light, spur people on to faith, remind them of the great love of Christ that is always there, and the promise of a relationship with the One who is victorious over all! Yes, this is your identity in Christ—a beautiful sweet aroma that is forever upon you and that lingers wherever you go! You are a blessing dear Daughter, and let this promise fill you with joy forevermore as it is your truest identity in Christ—*A Sweet Aroma.*

Prayer: Dear Jesus, thank you for the heavenly aroma you have given me that is pleasing to the Father! May people notice this and be reminded how much you love them as the aroma of your presence is powerfully lifechanging! In Jesus' name, Amen

31

WORTH DYING FOR

"but God shows his love for us in that while we were still sinners, Christ died for us."

ROMANS 5:8 ESV

When I was almost ten months pregnant, the time came for my first born to meet the world! I was excited, nervous, and in a lot of discomfort! I can remember those moments during labor when I really had to push through the natural pain of childbirth to look ahead to the joy that would come through motherhood. The temporary pain a mother endures is quickly replaced with love, joy, and comfort the moment she gets to meet her blessing from God and hold that little miracle.

Beloved Daughter of God, your Heavenly Father created all things in this world and called it good. God is outside of time and can see all things past, present and future. His perspective is one that can always overlook the temporary to see the eternal good that He has planned. When God sent His One and Only Son to this earth to take your place for punishment from sin and death, it was worth it all. Jesus said he was able to endure the cross, scorning its shame, for the joy set before him. Did you know that you, dear daughter, were that joy he thought about? Yes, he saw you, and said it was worth it all. You were worth dying for. No matter what you have done in the past, no matter how many times you have rejected him, doubted him, been mad at him…you were still worth it…and still are. His precious shed blood covers you like the beautiful flowers God created cover the earth. His shed blood for your sins was out of joy for you. Every time you see a cross, know that it was pure joy for your Savior to take the place for you so you could be with him forever in eternity. Reject all shame, lies you have believed, and self-condemnation because you are more precious than jewels to your Father. For this is your truest identity as a Beloved Daughter of God—*Worth Dying For!*

Prayer: Forgive me Father for any lies I have believed that I wasn't worth your love. Thank you for this new and secure identity of love. Thank you that when you died on the cross, you thought of me and said I was worth it! I love you! In Jesus' name. Amen!

KNOWN BY GOD

"You have searched me, Lord, and you know me."

PSALM 139:1 NIV

Locals of the quiet creeks of Murrells Inlet, SC know that at high tide each day, if you have a jon boat, you can have some fun riding around in the "mazes." The mazes are the beautiful pattern the marsh grass makes on the waters of the inlet. Most spots are not deep enough to drive a boat through until the waters of the tide are high enough that they cover the tops of the marsh grass and all you can see is green tips poking out of the calm salt water. Fortunately, I know a guy (my dear hubby) who has traveled these creeks his whole life. He knows them back and forth that he could probably drive the mazes blindfolded. He knows where to go along the inlet, when to turn, and how to get through this marvelous water puzzle our Heavenly Father created.

Beloved Daughter of God, you are known by your Heavenly Father. He has thought of you since the beginning of time and once you were conceived, He knit you together in your mother's womb. He knows when you sit down and when you rise up. He knows your thoughts and words even before they are formed. He knows you are going out and lying down. He knows you and everything about you, because He created you from a heart of pure agape love. Greater than any human could have knowledge of another, God knows you. And He accepts you with welcome arms, today and always. Don't ever let the lies of the enemy make you feel unseen, unheard, unknown or unloved. God sees you in your rejoicing and sorrow. God hears the praises and cries for help. Every part of your being is known to Him. Let this journey called life, be filled with joy and peace as you go through the twists and turns in life knowing that if God is the driver of the boat, He already knows what's ahead and where to go. No matter how complicated the pattern of the mazes of the marshes in your life, God knows how to get through, and with a lot of fun!! For this is your truest identity, Beloved Daughter of God, "Known by Him."

Prayer: Thank you Father that you see me and love me just as I truly am. What a peace I will walk in daily knowing I don't have to impress you, hide from you, or be something other than I am. Thank you that you abundantly love me beyond what my mind understands! I love you too!!

PROTECTED BY ANGEL ARMIES

"For He will command His angels concerning you, to guard you in all your ways."

PSALM 91:11 NIV

Have you ever driven through a tunnel made of trees? Growing up in South Carolina and frequently visiting the coastal areas of the Lowcountry, it is commonplace to drive through the beautiful covering of Live Oak trees. These ancient trees of some hundreds of years old provide an abundant shelter as the large thick branches connect on either side of the road and guard you from above. It's almost as if they are an army of soldiers lining the streets to confidently guard any passerby from harm. Mysterious in nature, these trees almost seem to be created by God as a special covering for His children. (Psalm 91:11)

Beloved Daughter of God, JEHOVAH-SABAOTH will protect you. Yes, God Almighty is the host of the armies of Heaven and will command them to help and protect you. You are His beloved, daughter of King Most High, brought by the blood of Jesus and cherished among all creation. Just as the beautiful live oak trees provide shelter and protection for those who travel underneath, you are in the palm of your Father's hand. Dwell in the shelter and rest in refuge of His protection. As you love the Lord your God with all your heart and trust in His promises, you stand protected under the fortress of His mighty embrace. Walk confidently each day knowing your powerful Father God is even stronger than the mightiest of trees that shelter the Lowcountry paths. Grasp ahold of this truth, as it is your truest identity as a Beloved Daughter of God—*Protected by Angel Armies.*

Prayer: Thank you God Almighty and Heavenly Father for your constant protection! I will choose to walk in faith trusting your loving Hand sheltering me from all evil schemes targeted against me. Even when my eyes make me want to fear, I will praise you all the more that you are at work in a great way that I cannot see. You are a good Father, and I am loved by you!

STRENGTHENED

"I can do all things through Christ who strengthens me."

PHILIPPIANS 4:13 NIV

What a great feeling it is to wake up in the morning feeling refreshed and strengthened from a good night's sleep. Have you ever felt so good, you have said the words, "I feel like a new person!"? Or how strengthening is the refreshment from rest after a vacation? Time at the beach, along the creek, a quiet river or a peaceful marsh? Sit back for a moment and think about how strength comes from rest. Obviously, our physical bodies need sleep at night to function normally each day. Our body needs rest to be strong. Most people would argue that going to the gym and lifting weights make your body strong; and I would agree. However, I would also argue that at the core of physical strength, rest is the most important.

Beloved Daughter of God, there is a strength that is necessary for survival that only your Heavenly Father can give you. This strength is more powerful than physical, mental, or emotional strength. No matter how hard you try to attain this, only God can give it to you. The good news is that He freely and abundantly gives it! It is out of this strength that all other strengths flow. Spending time with the Lord each morning, resting in His loving embrace is where true strength comes from. Praying and listening for His whispers of love is what refreshes your soul. Remembering what He has done in your life, and praising Him all the more builds faith that strengthens you for days to come. Seeking Him above all and committing to trust Him even when you don't understand, paves the way for great strength that no man can take from you. It's like a vacation for your inner-most being. Realizing you have a best friend in Jesus Christ that is walking alongside of you, who sympathizes with anything you might experience, fills you with strength, courage and boldness! It is Almighty God that strengthens you, and through whom you can do all things! This, dear sister, is your truest identity as a Beloved Daughter of God—*Strengthened!*

Prayer: Almighty God and Father, your strength is immeasurable and infinite! Any time I feel weak, remind me to press back into you, the source of all strength and power to be recharged! Thank you for your Word and promise that I truly can do all things through Christ who strengthens me!

GOD'S MASTERPIECE

"For we are God's masterpiece. He has created us anew in Christ Jesus,
so we can do the good things he planned for us long ago."

EPHESIANS 2:10 NLT

Growing up I was surrounded by art—surrounded by masterpieces that caring, sensitive, creative hands purposefully created. My mother and grandmother were both artists and their lives reflected the beauty of creating things in every manner. Whether it was cooking up a well thought out delicious meal, joyfully singing melodious songs, designing beautiful custom-made clothing, or spending hours in front of a blank white canvas transforming it into a magnificent work of art, I was able to witness first-hand the intentional hands of a creator and the resulting beautiful created masterpiece.

Beloved Daughter of God, did you know that you are valued more than any precious thing on this earth? Did you know that long ago, your Heavenly Father had a very special plan to create you anew in His image as His masterpiece? So many times, we allow comparison to rob us of the celebration of who God created us to be. Culture definitely has a set formula and standard of what its masterpiece looks like, and if you do not fit into that mold, then you are set back, unnoticed, and made to feel less than special. The truth is the Creator of all there is and ever will be, carefully and purposefully planned out everything about you and said that is was good.

Every day He rejoices over you with singing as He celebrates who you are. Don't ever criticize the beautiful, perfect and unique masterpiece that you alone are, but instead, embrace fully all that you are in Christ! You are truly a work of art constantly worth celebrating regardless of what anyone else says. See yourself from the perspective of the one who intricately designed you and resist all other viewpoints that lack His vision, because this dear one is your truest identity—God's Masterpiece!

Prayer: Precious Heavenly Father, thank you for creating me exactly like I am! Forgive me for condemning any part of myself, for you created me with loving hands for a great unique purpose. Today I choose to celebrate all that I am to you alone, Your Masterpiece. In Jesus' name, Amen!

SET FREE

"It is for freedom that Christ has set us free. Stand firm then and do not let yourselves be burdened again by a yoke of slavery."

GALATIANS 5:1 NIV

Our favorite family dog was a Labrador Retriever named Scout. From a young age, my husband worked with him very closely to train him to become the excellently behaved companion who loved to walk, run and bird hunt. His master, my husband, set him free from his wild puppy nature and trained him so that he would walk right beside us when we went on a long jog in the neighborhood or retrieve a bird from across the pond in a flash of time just with a one word command.

Beloved Daughter of God, you too have been set free in the most glorious way from the death producing sin nature and yoke of slavery that you were born with. Jesus took the yoke of slavery upon himself, nailed it to the cross and defeated the power of sin and death when he arose again! You aren't trapped by the religious fence of condemnation from your sinful nature anymore. You have been set free and are able to walk in complete freedom to follow the righteous life Jesus has for you that leads to abundant, joyful, peaceful and eternal life now and forever! Once slave to sin and death, but now free to walk in obedience in following Christ that leads to fulfilling the amazing purpose and destiny God planned out for you long ago. This is good news and it is your truest identity as a Beloved Daughter of God, Set Free!

Prayer: Dear Heavenly Father, thank you for your perfect plan of salvation that I am able to be set free in Christ to walk in obedience and righteousness. Help me continually stand firm again the old self and walk boldly and confidently by your Spirit that leads to continual freedom!

A POWERFUL COMPANION

"The Spirit of God, who raised Jesus from the dead, lives in you."

ROMANS 8:11 NLT

The first time I flew in an airplane was exhilarating! The airplane gave me the ability to do what I could not do myself—fly! What was humanly impossible now became possible in a flash of time. Endless opportunities opened up, new mindsets about the world raced through my mind, and hopes and dreams were ignited.

Beloved Daughter of God, did you know you have been given a miraculous gift so much better than the ability to fly? Before Jesus left this earth, he promised to send you a powerful companion, the Holy Spirit. All worry, fear and hopelessness have been destroyed as love conquered all and sent you the Spirit of Truth to help you and be with you forever! This powerful companion, the Holy Spirit, is here to walk alongside you on this path of life. Take time to listen for the One who has not left you alone but is right by your side. Yes, your companion is the greatest comforter, advocate, and helper and is only a breath away. He is not silent, but you must eagerly listen for His loving and generous whispers of truth that will break every chain the enemy tries to entangle you with. As you spend time with him and become more aware of His constant presence, you will be empowered with a bold confidence that nothing is impossible with Him! The same Spirit that raised Jesus from the dead is alive in you, dear daughter. Our powerful comforter will equip you with everything you need to fulfill the great purpose you were created for. This blessed truth is your truest identity as a Beloved Daughter of God, given—*A Powerful Companion!*

Prayer: Thank you Heavenly Father for giving me Your Holy Spirit to be my powerful companion now and forever. I choose this day to believe this truth and walk in confidence that I have everything I need to overcome any obstacle with your Holy Spirit guiding me into all truth.

FRUITFUL

"I am the vine; you are the branches. If you remain in me and I in you,
you will bear much fruit; apart from me you can do nothing."

JOHN 15:5 NIV

When I first became a Christian, I studied the Bible to find out this new way I was supposed to live. Since my old self had gone, and my new self-had come through salvation, I needed to know what "rules" I needed to follow. What do Christians do, or should I say not do? Over time, that led me further from relationship, and more towards pursuing works to feel like I was pleasing God. Striving to please God left me dry inside and vulnerable to believing lies about my identity in Christ.

Beloved Daughter of God, your Heavenly Father doesn't want you to follow a bunch of rules, but instead seek Him in relationship and respond to follow Him wherever He leads. A life of striving to do good works will leave you empty and exhausted. Instead, just stay close to Jesus and follow where God's Holy Spirit leads. This is where the adventure, fun, and abundance flow out of! Just like a beautiful lake nourishes all the plants and vegetation around it to be fruitful and flourish, you were made to be fruitful on the inside and out. You were made to flourish! You were created to let His love fill you up to overflowing each day, and then get released in powerful fruit for you and others. Jesus said that all you need to do is remain in him and he in you and you will bear much fruit! Yes, the result of this relationship is a promise from Galatians 5—love, joy, peace patience, kindness, goodness, faithfulness, gentleness and self-control. It's your irrevocable right as a Daughter of God. Anytime you feel "fruitless," just remember Jesus is only a whisper away. Press back into him in worship, praise, prayer, and fellowship and as you realign yourself in his love, you will again see that beautiful fruit blessing you and everyone God puts in your path. This dear sister is your truest identity as a beloved Daughter of God: Fruitful!"

Prayer: Jesus, thank you that my right as a Daughter of God is to be fruitful. Help me today to remain completely in you so that I will bear much fruit. I want to be filled completely to overflowing so that I may spill over on to each person you place in my life today. Not in my own strength, but always yours. Amen.

REJOICED OVER

"The Lord your God is with you, the Mighty Warrior who saves,
he will take great delight in you and he will rejoice over you with singing."

ZEPHANIAH 3:17 NIV

One of my absolute favorite things to do is to walk outside and notice all of nature working together in perfect unison. The birds are happy singing their beautiful melodious tunes, the sun shining down nourishing all plants and providing warmth and light to all living things, rushing rivers and calm streams offering refreshment, people going about their day and so much more. Everything seems to have a buzz of delight about it, as if it were marked at the core with rejoicing from a loving Creator since the beginning of time.

Beloved Daughter of God, did you know your Heavenly Father delighted to the fullest extent when he created you in your mother's womb? Since time began, God has rejoiced over everything he created, calling it very good. He was full of joy after fearfully and wonderfully creating you completely different and unique than anyone else in this world. Sometimes it is easy to lose sight of this when we face trials and rejection from the world. Don't for one moment partner with the lie that you are anything less than spectacular, because the truth is you can only be correctly valued by the One made you. Your Father God takes great delight in you and rejoices over you, regardless of what you have or what you've done; You are rejoiced over because of who you are, an image bearer of the Mighty Warrior who saves, passionately loved more than all other living things on this earth. Remember this daily and walk confidently knowing your truest identity—Rejoiced Over.

Prayer: Heavenly Father, what a comforting truth to know that when you think of me, your heart bursts with delight. I choose to believe and walk in this glorious assurance that my identity in you is, Rejoiced Over. In Jesus' name, Amen.

RIGHTEOUS

"God made him who had no sin to be sin for us, so that in him we might become the righteousness of God."

2 Corinthians 5:21 NIV

Growing up I can remember my mom hand-making a beautiful white dress for me to wear on Easter Sunday when I was eight. I was so excited about wearing it because not only was it carefully designed with love, but I felt so special wearing it! After a lovely church service remembering the amazing gift Jesus gave us on the cross, our family celebrated with a big Easter brunch.

Within minutes of my first bite, I spilled ketchup on this white dress. I was so upset that I ruined my new dress, however, my mom reassured me that this miraculous product called Bleach could take away all stain so that it would be perfect again!

Beloved Daughter of God, the finished work Jesus did on the cross is like our spiritual bleach! When Jesus became your Lord and Savior, a powerful and permanent removal of your sin-stained heart took place. Now and forever when God looks at you, He sees the One that is in you who took your sins away. He sees your Savior, His Son, Jesus, who is perfect in every way. No matter what you have done or will do in the future can stain or taint your right standing with God. When He removed all sin, He also removed all shame, guilt, fear, and condemnation. You are no longer a slave to sin, nor is there any condemnation since you are in the body of Christ. He clothed you in purple robes of righteousness, no longer an orphan, but a righteous daughter of God. Let this truth permeate every area of your heart and mind. Say aloud, "I am God's beloved daughter, pure, righteous and clean because of my Lord Jesus!" Destroy any lie, doubt, worry or fear that tries to deceive you into believing anything will separate you from the love of God. Your Father adores you and as He lovingly looks upon you, He sees the perfect One whom you are in, Christ Jesus. For this is your truest identity as a Beloved Daughter of God—*Righteous.*

Prayer: Thank you Jesus for taking away all my sin and shame. I will joyously walk in my identity as righteous knowing there is nothing I can ever do to lose this hope and assurance.

SEEN BY GOD

"Behold, the eye of the Lord is on those who fear Him, On those who hope in His mercy."

PSALM 33:18 NKJV

Searching for a tiny shark's tooth on the beautiful sandy beaches of South Carolina is one of my favorite activities when my family vacations each summer. It is amazing that even amidst the crushed bits and pieces of seashells and everything else found on the soft sand, when your eye is trained to find a shark's tooth, they are easy to spot. My kids and I come home with pockets full of all sizes of black & brown shark's teeth! What a treasure they are to find knowing they came from a mysterious and powerful sea creature!

Beloved Daughter of God, even amidst all the people that occupy this earth, God sees you. He created you fearfully and wonderfully, loves you greater than the distance of the east and west, and knows you so intricately He can count the hairs on your head! Sometimes your emotions will lead you into believing you are all alone, or that God isn't listening when you pray to Him, or He has so many children to care for that you are forgotten. This could not be further from the truth.

His loving eye is trained to spot you—unique one of a kind you—amongst all people. When you arise in the morning, He is there with you singing praises over you, when you draw near to Him in prayer He is ever so near, and even when you have turned away from Him, He's there. He is with you always, and as you continually choose Him as Lord and Savior, His eye never leaves your sight. He chose you first, and He will continue to choose you each and every day for the rest of your life. You are secure in His steadfast love, one that cannot be earned nor ever taken away. Embrace this peaceful promise of comfort that is your truest identity as a Beloved Daughter of God—*Seen By God.*

Prayer: Thank you Father that you see me. Even when I feel all alone, I will trust in the promise of your constant presence. You are with me, you see me and you are always at work to help work all things out for my good and your glory. In Jesus' name, Amen.

SHEPHERDED TENDERLY

"The Lord is my Shepherd, I lack nothing."

PSALM 23:1 NIV

Have you ever felt out of control? Maybe things weren't going the way you wanted, but instead looked scary or hopeless. You felt alone, trapped, and afraid. When my firstborn was an infant, she came down with a horrible respiratory infection. After rounds of antibiotics, she wasn't getting better and the pathway to her lungs was so irritated she had trouble breathing. As a new mom, I didn't know how to care for her and it was one of the scariest moments of my life.

Beloved Daughter of God, the good news is that you are not in control. The One who is in control, is a good Shepherd who cares so tenderly for you. Those moments you feel out of control should be a reminder to pause, surrender the situation to the Lord, and thank Him that in His care He will work it all out for your good and His glory. Yes, dear one, you are loved beyond measure by a Shepherd who has all the resources of Heaven at His fingertips. He will provide whatever He sees as best for you that you need moment by moment. Sometimes, those are provisions of faith, strength, peace, love, joy or whatever else is most important for you in the moment. He promises to provide what you need as you trust Him. Your Shepherd is not only a promise maker but a promise keeper. So, rejoice as you follow Him closely trusting He will always be there for you. For this is your truest identity as a Beloved Daughter of God—*Shepherded Tenderly.*

Prayer: Thank you Jesus that you are my Good Shepherd. What a comfort it brings me to know I am loved beyond measure, and I can rest in your loving arms at all times. Give me strength this day and always to have your deep inner peace to live by faith knowing you are always at work for my good and your glory.

ALL THINGS WORK TOGETHER FOR GOOD

"And we know that in all things God works for the good of those who love him, who have been called according to his purpose."

ROMANS 8:28 NIV

Mistakes, disappointments, hardships, trials, disobedience, failures—sometimes, it's hard to believe God can really turn things that seem really bad into good. For seven long years I was in a tough season. It felt like God had turned His ear from me as all prayers I lifted up had no visible answer. This season was called "Wait." If you are anything like me, when you get your mind set on something, you want it…and want it now.

Beloved Daughter of God, did you know that God's ways are truly higher and better than you could ever imagine? Did you know that there is a great purpose for every season of life you go through. In the Fall season of life when everything seems to be changing like the color of leaves do in nature, or in the cold lonely winter seasons of life when things seem dead or asleep, God is working. God is preparing you for the season of Springtime. Your eyes just cannot see or mind believe what is going on beneath the soil in your life. Every time you give God your situation, your trial, or your hurts, He will work it out. It's not just a hopeful thought to ease the pain, but a powerful promise that will change your life if you choose to believe it. Look for God's hand in every moment of your life…it's there. When you cannot see His hand, then trust His heart. It is to love you, and to mold you into the amazing Daughter He created you to become. Oh, and if you get "stuck" in that season of NO or Wait, then get excited because He is at work in the unseen and His beautiful creation will be revealed as you press into His love. Be thankful God doesn't seek your advice on timing, because in your timing, you aren't ready for His gifts. In your timing, you will spoil the good gifts He has for you. It's in the process, in the changing of seasons, in waiting on Him that you will be able to see His glorious master plan where all things work together for your good and His glory. Stand firm in this rich privilege of allowing God to work all things out. That, dear sister is your truest identity as a Beloved Daughter of God—*All things working together for good.*

Prayer: Heavenly Father, your plan is perfect. Forgive me for the times I have doubted your ways or timing. Thank you for loving me more than my mind can fathom, and always working for my good as I trust and love you.

SET APART

"Know that the Lord has set apart his faithful servant for himself; the Lord hears when I call to him."

PSALM 4:3 NIV

When I married my husband many years ago, I did what many brides do and took on his last name as my own. As I honored my parents and the legacy they had given me, I had now taken on a brand-new identity between God and my husband as wife and a member of his namesake. This blessed unity had set me apart from my prior identity as I stepped into something new, exciting and of God.

Beloved Daughter of God, when you became the bride of Christ, everything changed. Under his lordship, protection, provision and body, God set you apart for His righteous purposes. God called you out of the darkness and into His wonderful light. Your identity has now become one that sets you apart with Heavenly privileges and rights. You may not look any different than you did before Christ, but you are! You are now within the body of Christ—an irrevocable identity.

Walking by faith and not sight alone allows you to see from God's perspective on how He can work all things for good according to His purposes. He continually fills you with His love and every other good thing so that you can be a light for all to see and His hands and feet to love others. You are His workmanship, set apart to do good works through Jesus. Following His Word is your guide to stay within the loving boundaries to carry out the work He created you for. Beautiful abundant and fragrant fruit of His Holy Spirit will be the result of your daily walk with your loving Father. You are set apart for great things dear Daughter and you are set apart for a loving intimate relationship with Him. Call out to Him often and listen back for His gentle and peaceful whispers of love. For this is your truest identity as a Beloved Daughter of God—*Set Apart.*

Prayer: Thank you God for setting me apart as your child. I receive this identity and will walk confidently knowing I am yours forever and you are at work in and through me in a mighty way. Give me ears to hear you more clearly and a heart that patiently awaits your leading. In Jesus' name, Amen.

EMPOWERED

"And if the Spirit of him who raised Jesus from the dead is living in you, he who raised Christ from the dead will also give life to your mortal bodies because of his Spirit who lives in you."

ROMANS 8:11 NIV

When I was a little girl, I found great strength and encouragement from my sweet mama. In the night, when I awoke abruptly from a bad dream, calling for my mother and knowing she was there to help brought comfort. Or when I was older and I would compete in sports, she would always cheer me on from the sidelines which brought an inner strength and confidence that propelled me onward and upward. Over the years, she has been there to lend her ear and offer great wisdom as life has taken its twists and turns, which have been the biggest blessing of encouragement and empowerment.

Beloved Daughter of God, did you realize that when you gave your life to Jesus Christ as Lord and Savior, God placed the same Holy Spirit that raised Christ from the dead inside of you? In an instant, you became empowered with His powerful and mighty Spirit! You may not look any different, or even feel different, but your Heavenly Father placed the "secret ingredient" in you to give you true abundant life forever!! You are empowered in life to walk in victory, faith, love, peace, joy, hope, security, and so much more! His Spirit is your companion to help you in every way and at any moment! Just like a boat is a tool to help you travel by water, God's powerful Spirit within you is a gift to empower you to live the abundant life God has planned out for you.

You have everything you need for the journey of life now with God's Spirit alive in you!! Infinitely better than any human can possibly help, comfort, or encourage you, God's powerful Spirit is in you to see to it that victory is realized. Take a moment now to embrace this truth, thank the Lord for His Spirit living in you, and feel empowered! Walk boldly and courageously along God's path for your life because of your powerful companion. This is your truest identity, beloved Daughter of God—*Empowered!* Begin each day with this reminder and walk it out in faith each moment!

Prayer: Thank you Father for the mighty gift of your Holy Spirit! I will walk empowered by the belief and knowledge that nothing shall be impossible with your powerful spirit guiding me. Give me a greater ability to hear you leading me so that I may fulfill the great purpose you created me for!

PRESENT WITH GOD

"Don't fear, because I am with you; don't be afraid, for I am your God. I will strengthen you,
I will surely help you; I will hold you with my righteous strong hand."

Isaiah 41:10 CEBA

A couple of summers ago, our family took a fun sun-filled Caribbean cruise vacation. On the third day we opted for an excursion which took us and a group of sixty other cruisers to a private island for the day to play, eat, snorkel, whatever our hearts' desired! All was well until my precious five year old son wandered off and got lost. The ten minutes he went missing was one of the scariest moments of both his and our lives.

Beloved Daughter of God, as you walk along the path of life, you may feel fear. You may not know where you are going. You may get discouraged as the path of life takes twists and turns. Even if you feel like you have lost your way, there is hope. There is good news beloved! God is always present with you! The assurance of His presence brings peace and security. His presence kills all FEAR and discouragement! God tells us repeatedly throughout scripture, that He will be with us. Before Jesus left this earth, he told his disciples, "I will be with you always" (Matthew 28:20). It is so important to realize that your truest identity in Christ is "Present with Him," even when you feel like my son who was all alone and scared because he wandered off and got lost. You are never alone, because God is always present with you through His amazing Holy Spirit. That presence is His gift of strength, confidence, courage, peace, security, and love. Your identity, beloved daughter, is not "alone and a worrier" but "present with God and a warrior" because God is ALWAYS present with you! Every time you feel afraid, hit the pause button on your life and acknowledge this important truth. Say out loud, "God is with me and I am not afraid!" Remember that He is right beside you, holding your hand on the path He created just for you. This is your truest identity—*Present with God.*

Prayer: Dear Heavenly Father, though I cannot see you, I believe your Word that you are with me always. Help me walk boldly wherever you lead as I trust your loving guidance. I declare that you are Almighty God over all things and are constantly with me, so I resist all fear and remain securely in your loving embrace!

FEARLESS

"There is no fear in love. Instead, perfect love drives fear away."

1 John 4:18 NIRV

When I was in the fifth grade, I went on a class trip with my elementary school to a camp up in the mountains for three days. My favorite memory from that trip was completing the "trust falls" with my small group. I stood on a ledge about eight feet high, facing backwards and eyes closed, as my friends and teachers were below with arms wide open ready to catch me as I trusted them and fell back. As I fell back into what felt completely unknown and unsecure, I was fearful. But before I hit the ground, I experienced the greatest feeling of love as strong hands of those below caught me. What seemed like the scariest moment of my life turned into one of my greatest lessons of love. How exhilarating to reject the fear of falling (and not understanding), and trust I would be caught by hands of love!

Beloved Daughter of God, you are so abundantly loved. Did you know that you are in the palm of God's hand? Did you realize that the One who created you loves you so much and will not leave you nor forsake you? In Christ, your identity is fearless because His perfect love drives out all fear. You can trust in the Lord with all your heart and lean not on your own understanding and He will make every path straight for you. Sometimes, your life may seem like you are standing backwards, eyes closed and falling into the unknown and unsecure. It may feel like you are walking blindly or even alone. But you can be assured, that the Lord, yes the Host of Heaven is there to not only catch you but love you. He is there to walk alongside you and make the darkness light. It is His love that is the most powerful force of all nature! Anytime you feel fear trying to come upon you or even overtake you, remember who you are to your Heavenly Father and also who it is that is standing behind you to catch you!! That perfect love of His will send that fear as far as the east is from the west and you will be comforted by His peace. Claim your truest identity—*Daughter of God*—and walk in it, for you ARE fearless!!

Prayer: Dear Heavenly Father, I declare aloud that in You I am fearless! All fear from doubt and worry must flee now in Jesus' name, as I remain completely in my Daddy's perfect love. Thank you Lord Jesus, for making a way for me to be in you as everything is under your feet! I will walk in bold confidence clinging to my sword, your Word! In Jesus' name, Amen!

THE DEVIL FLEES FROM ME

"Submit yourselves, then, to God. Resist the devil, and he will flee from you."

JAMES 4:7 NIV

My favorite part of the day is early morning before sunrise. It takes my breath away to watch how God faithfully awakens each day by making the darkness of night flee with the unfailing rising of the sun breaking through bringing light to all creation. The light and love of Almighty God upon this earth in His powerful creation of light causes darkness to flee and the light of life to prevail.

Beloved Daughter of God, even more powerful than the burning light of the sun is the resurrection power of Christ living in you. Once you submitted yourself to Father God and Jesus Christ as Lord and Savior, everything changed within you. You became a new creation in Christ, not ruled by the laws of this world anymore, but having the blood of Christ running through your veins and permanently placed in the body of Christ in which everything in all creation is below his feet. It is now your right as a child of God to have power over sin and darkness as Christ is head over all power and authority that exists. Just as the sunlight of each day pierces the darkness, anytime you experience darkness coming against you, exercise your authority in Christ. Stand firm in your faith in God and resist it, and your inheritance is the promise of all darkness must bow to Christ and flee. Submit to the Lord in prayer, worship, claiming scripture or however the Holy Spirit leads you, and darkness must flee. What an exhilarating promise that is! Believe this truth and walk boldly in this identity that was generously bestowed upon you. For this is your truest identity in Christ—*The Devil Flees From Me.*

Prayer: Thank you Father for the authority you have given me in Christ as your Beloved Daughter. Let this promise permeate my heart and mind so that I may boldly walk on the path you have set before me, so that nothing can stand in the way. In Jesus' name, Amen.

OVERCOMER

"For everyone who has been born of God overcomes the world.
This is the victory that has overcome the world—our faith."

1 JOHN 5:4 NIV

I love stories of a comeback—stories where the underdog, the one who looked like he had no chance of winning or surviving, persevered and pushed against all odds and did it. We see this in every aspect of life: in business, sports, health, relationships, all facets of everyday life. Doesn't victory seem even sweeter when the underdog wins? Isn't it even more thrilling when the weak beat the strong? We see this all throughout the Bible…Moses and Pharaoh, David and Goliath, Joshua and the giants in the Promised Land, Daniel and the Lion's Den…. the Bible is made up on underdogs. The greatest underdog of all that no one saw coming was Jesus Christ.

Beloved Daughter of God take a moment right now to praise God! Lift your hands up and give the Lord all glory and honor as He is the greatest victor of all time! Jesus lived a sinless life, defeated death on a cross, and rose from the dead! No one in all of history can boast such a powerful victory! The best news of all is that He does not keep the victory for himself alone. No, once you put your faith in Christ as Lord and Savior, you too get to share in His victory too! Yes, the greatest victory of all time gets to be your story too. Not only was it a one-time victory, but His resurrection changed everything as it set the precedent for victory to be the standard for those in Christ! Isn't that the best news yet? This is your new normal and forever identity!

When you feel defeated, remind yourself of this truth and let your faith in Christ fill you with confident assurance once again. You can do all things through Christ who strengthens you! You are more than a conqueror through Him who loved you. Jesus said with faith you can even command the mountains to move! Yes, and amen! Receive this truth anew and be refreshed that no matter what underdog moments you experience in life, in Christ you will always win! For this is your truest identity as a Beloved Daughter of God—*Overcomer.*

Prayer: Thank you God that I am and will always be an overcomer! Thank you that there is no mountain too high, nor valley too low, with you by my side anything is possible! I receive this identity as an Overcomer now and forever. In Jesus' name, Amen.

STRONG AND COURAGEOUS

Haven't I commanded you? Strength! Courage! Don't be timid; don't get discouraged. God, your God, is with you every step you take."

Joshua 1:9 MSG

In 2018, God showed me glimpses of the Promised Land He was giving me to enjoy, occupy, and be blessed by. It looked amazing. It was a land I knew would be not only desirable, but also fulfill my deepest desires and bring about my greatest gifts. However, it also looked quite scary as there were so many unknowns, so many questions, so many leaps of faith required to enter into this land, conquer it, and occupy it. God was giving me the greatest gift of my life, yet also calling me to dig deeper than I ever had to find great strength and courage to receive this gift. The choice I had to make was—did I trust He would be with me and help me?

Beloved Daughter of God, throughout your whole life, your Heavenly Father has been preparing you to enter into His amazing promised land. He has been teaching you little by little how to walk stronger each day to prepare you for the journey. God has commanded you to be strong and courageous only because He put tremendous strength and courage inside of you and desires to bring it forth for your good and to be a display of His splendor. He is calling you to trust Him, trust in His presence with you, and trust in His provision as you set forth on this epic journey called life. He is calling you to be strong and courageous and look ahead where He is leading.

He will give you victory when you look to Him instead of looking at any giants in the land that seek to make you afraid. He is the victor and He is with you. As you walk boldly and courageously into the promised land, He will grow you into a mighty Oak of Righteousness. Trust Him and step out boldly in faith and see your truest identity as Beloved Daughter of God revealed—*Strong and Courageous!*

Prayer: Dear Heavenly Father, thank you that you call me to be strong and courageous! I choose this and every new day to walk by courage only because I know you are with me. Where you call me to go, I will go, for I know you will never leave me but will help me overcome any giant no matter how big or how scary it looks. You are above all, and I am completely in you! In Jesus' mighty name, Amen!

CONFIDENT IN GOD

"For the Lord will be your confidence and will keep your foot from being caught."

PROVERBS 3:26 ESV

Several years ago, I took the biggest leaf of faith in my life. God called me to leave my successful career as an Insurance Advisor and go on an unknown adventure with Him. Yes, when He called me to take this leap of faith, I did not yet know at the time what I was actually "leaping" into! The only thing I did know was that He put a burning passion deep in my heart for something and I had to trust Him to find out what that was. I had to be confident in Him.

Beloved Daughter of God, your Heavenly Father loves you. He has great plans for you. Sometimes those plans look uncertain, unknown and quite scary. Your faith is tested and strengthened when you put your confidence in the Lover of your soul and follow where He is leading you. Philippians 1:6 encourages us that God will finish the good work that He began in you when you accepted Jesus Christ as Lord and Savior. Your truest identity is a "Confident Daughter of God!" Yes, when you follow Him, you can hold your head high, walking tall and strong knowing that even if you can't see where the next step will lead you, GOD is your confidence and will lead you to fulfilling the great purpose He created you for! You can be CONFIDENT that the Lord is at your side. You can be CONFIDENT that the Lord will be your security. You can be CONFIDENT that God will be your peace! When life's uncertainties make you want to stand still and stop moving, just remember you can be confident and take that LEAP of faith wherever He is leading you. You can be CONFIDENT because God is faithful. He's faithful to all of His creation as proven with the never failing rising and setting of the sun each day. God will never let His creation down, but will always be faithful! I can testify to you now years later that leaping in confidence with God and risking everything was the best decision I have ever made! You can do this too, because the Lord IS your confidence!! Beloved Daughter of God, this is your truest identity—*Confident in God!*

Prayer: Thank you Almighty God that you are my complete confidence! I will choose to walk boldly each and every new day because I know you are with me every step of the way! Give me ears to hear you and eyes to see you and a pure heart to follow you, for your perfect way is my heart's delight! In Jesus' name, Amen!

IMMEASURABLY LOVED

"And I pray that you, being rooted and established in love, may have power, together with all the Lord's holy people, to grasp how wide and long and high and deep is the love of Christ, and to know this love that surpasses knowledge—that you may be filled to the measure of all the fullness of God."

EPHESIANS 3:17B-19 NIV

Have you ever been a little chilly and walked outside to warm up by sitting in the warm sunshine? Very quickly as your body absorbs the powerful sunlight, your once cold restricted skin relaxes as it takes in the calming yet powerful rays of sunshine filling you with warmth, peace and strength. Just the posture of receiving the warm beautiful sunlight connects deeply to every part of your body as well as beautifies every single created thing around you!

Beloved Daughter of God, come sit in the warmth of His presence, as your Heavenly Father invites you to receive your truest identity as immeasurably loved. Yes, life seems cold at times and your body can easily tense up and become stressed. At the foundation of every thought and mindset, make this truth your core message. God lovingly thought of you, created you, and formed you in your mother's womb in love. You have been firmly rooted in His love, and this is a love that you cannot even comprehend, but you must completely believe and receive. This love that God has for you, that He also placed in you, and you are privileged to powerfully pass on to others changes everything. It's the love of Christ that was willing to give up a heavenly crown, face trials and persecution, and sacrifice his life so that you would know and believe first hand that you are immeasurably loved. God is always thinking lovingly towards you and watching over your life as Father. Spend time thinking of how your Father is constantly showing His love to you—how He helps you, provides for you, surprises you with good things, leads you with creative ideas, fills you with joy, give you discipline, structure and order, protects you, puts other people in your life at the right time, continually connects you to Him, and created a beautiful world for you to enjoy. If you can surrender trying to understand this love in your mind and just receive it fully in your heart, it will bless you just like sitting in that beautiful warm sunshine. It will change everything. Receive your truest identity now and forever as a Beloved Daughter of God—*Immeasurably Loved.*

Prayer: Dear Daddy in Heaven, thank you that you love me with a love I can never lose. Your constant unchanging love is my complete security in life. If you love me completely, I will never lack anything. I receive this identity as immeasurably loved and I love you too! In Jesus' name, Amen.

FILLED WITH JOY

"I have told you this so that my joy may be in you and that your joy may be complete."

John 15:11 NIV

Spring is my favorite time of the year! As the earth comes back to life from its long winter's nap, flowers burst open with beautiful fragrant blooms, birds joyously sing, and the Lord's warm blanket covers the earth once again. It seems the springtime sun fills the earth with joy and all the earth responds with rejoicing!

Beloved Daughter of God, happiness ebbs and flows, but God's joy flowing in and through you is a constant promise you get to remain in daily! As you spend time with the Lord each day in worship, praise, prayer, and growing in the knowledge of His Word, a supernatural filling of joy miraculously takes place! God is joy and when you draw near to Him, He fills you with every good thing He is! What a beautiful truth that you get to be the recipient of His amazing love, peace, joy, strength, hope, etc. all the time! He has filled you with His powerful Holy Spirit and one of the beautiful fruits of that Spirit is joy! Take advantage of this beautiful truth and let it flow abundantly through you and out to others!! Joy is contagious, so give it out generously! If you ever feel your joy tank running on low, take a moment, put your eyes back on the One who is joy, and anything contrary to that joy will flee! His joy is abundant and unending!! You are God's beloved Daughter, so as heir, you have the inheritance of everything good He has! Declare this truth and walk it out with confidence, for this is your truest identity as a beloved Daughter of God—*Filled with Joy*!

Prayer: Thank you Jesus that you have given me great joy! Even if circumstances are not joyful, I will stay joyful because your love is enough! You are enough! Let me be filled so much to overflowing today that other people get filled with this beautiful joy too!! In Jesus' name, Amen.

BEAUTIFULLY CROWNED

"I will put beautiful crowns on their heads instead of ashes."

Isaiah 61:3 NIRV

When I was a little girl, I used to dream of one day becoming a princess beautifully crowned when that "happily ever after" would come and I met my Prince Charming. All the movies that little girls like helped to instill this inner desire of one day meeting that special someone who would cherish me, love me, and call me beautiful. However, my story is common. As life took its twists and turns, and through the ups and downs, that once desired crown of beauty felt more like painful ashes when hurts and wounds became the identity.

Beloved Daughter of God, hurt, pains and mistakes are NOT your identity. That dream of Prince Charming was put in your heart to spur you on to finding the true King of your heart, Jesus Christ. The good news is that he will take every hurt, pain, mistake, wound, and trauma and turn it into a crown of beauty. As you spend time with the King of your heart, beloved princess, he will make those scars look like beauty marks. Oh, how beautiful in His sight you are! Your heart's desire to be loved and cherished is fulfilled in spending time with the King of kings! Sometimes the ashes of life help us realize how amazing our King truly is and how He will use it ALL for good! God's miraculous ways are higher than the highest mountain and can turn any trial into a triumph! No matter what the setting of your life looks like now, under His Lordship the canvas of your life will become a magnificent masterpiece! Don't let the enemy lie to you anymore and rob you of your true identity. You are not marked with scars, but instead crowned with beauty in Christ alone! This is your truest identity—*Beautifully Crowned!*

Prayer: Dear Heavenly Father, you are the King of my heart. You are a good Father, and I am loved by you. I receive this new identity as your beloved princess, beautifully crowned by the blood of Jesus upon my life. Thank you that you are able to take all things in my life that the enemy intended for harm and use them as a beautiful testimony of your love and faithfulness!

AMBASSADOR OF CHRIST

"We are therefore Christ's ambassadors, as though God were making his appeal through us. We implore you on Christ's behalf: Be reconciled to God."

2 Corinthians 5:20 NIV

It is always exciting to see seasons change each year when the deadness of winter is awakened and made new with the emerging life that springtime brings. What was once dead comes alive and all human senses get engaged with delightful fragrances of beautiful flowers, breathtaking bright colors popping up, and the warm sunshine covering the earth like your favorite comfortable blanket.

Beloved Daughter of God, when you received Jesus as your Lord and Savior, you moved from winter to springtime in a flash of time. The old sinful nature died and you were made anew with your Heavenly Father's Holy Spirit, completely changed forever. God entrusts you as His precious child with everything that He is and has and you have been given the honor and privilege to represent your Daddy now and forever. Created in His image, you have been given the mind of Christ and empowered to go and do whatever mission He sends you on! His perfect love that casts out all fear fuels you to be His hands and feet administering His great gift of reconciliation everywhere you go. The powerful gifts of His love, peace, joy, forgiveness, patience, kindness, gentleness and self-control are your tools and weapons to powerfully represent God and love others in a way that brings about total life change. What a great gift your Heavenly Father has joyfully entrusted you with, for He loves you with an everlasting love that fills you up and overflows to others to spur them on. You are one of a kind—unique and created to specifically represent your Daddy in a beautiful way! Be confident in this blessed purpose as it is your truest identity as a Beloved Daughter of God—*an Ambassador of Christ*!

Prayer: What a blessed gift you have given me precious Lord and Savior! Thank you for making me new and alive in you! I receive this privileged role and position as daughter and Ambassador of Christ. I choose to partner with everything you are doing here and represent you well by loving others like you do!

DISCIPLINED

"For the Spirit God gave us does not make us timid,
but gives us power, love and self-discipline."

2 Timothy 1:7 NIV

My mother often tells me that when she spends time with the Lord Jesus each morning, she envisions meeting him on a park bench in a beautiful garden. She sets aside time each morning to see what adventure awaits as she quiets herself and the buzz of the world all around her and waits in this special place for Jesus to meet with her. This beautiful pattern of disciplined time with the Lord sets the foundation for her whole day as our amazing loving Savior daily renews and refreshes her entire being with what He sees she needs.

Beloved Daughter of God, as you fight against the "busyness" of life and quiet yourself to your Heavenly Father each day with the Spirit's beautiful fruit of discipline, a supernatural refreshment of His love, joy, peace, hope, faith, strength and so much more fills you back up. It is His presence that truly is the gift, and God has made a way through the gift of self-discipline to say yes to Him and no to other things that pale in comparison to this special time. You may not meet with Jesus on a park bench in a garden, but if you come near to Him, His Word promises that He will be near to you. It is of utmost importance that you spend daily time to reset so you are again reminded of your identity as a Beloved Daughter of God. As you stand in this beautiful identity of a disciplined child of God, timidity, fear and worry flee. The Spirit in you that gives you power, love and self-discipline works in you to look like your sweet Daddy in Heaven, a God of order, productivity and achieving purpose. You are able to freely and boldly walk in His promises set forth for you. Embrace and stay focused on these truths as you walk courageously in your truest identity–*Disciplined Beloved Daughter of God.*

Prayer: Dear Jesus, thank you for giving me a spirit of power, love and self-discipline. Help me stay focused completely on where you lead today and not get distracted on trivial things. Thank you that I can have a sweet assurance that you always have time for me as I humble myself before you. I love you! Amen.

GIFTED WITH SALVATION

"For God so loved the world that he gave his one and only Son,
that whoever believes in him shall not perish but have eternal life."

JOHN 3:16 NIV

Do you remember the anticipation of Christmas morning when you were a child? How exciting was the thought of opening that special gift from your parents or a loved one? Gifts are wonderful things. Careful thought goes into giving a special gift and is selected especially with the recipient's desires, needs, and wishes in mind. And there is no debt involved when receiving a gift as it is just a loving free exchange from one person to another.

Beloved Daughter of God, do you realize that you have been offered the most precious gift this life has to offer? Your loving Heavenly Father had a wonderful plan before the world began, and it included a relationship with you, His precious baby girl. He created you with a great purpose, and a plan to fulfill it by offering this special gift of salvation. It is a path of pure righteousness paved by the shed blood of Jesus Christ, leading to a blessed life full of joy, peace, hope, security, love, and so much more. You have been gifted with salvation, eternal security, and hope of a restored relationship with your Lord and Savior. The question is, have you received this identity? Have you received the gift of salvation? Your Father gives it freely no matter what your past or present looks like, no strings attached! Confess your sins to the One whose shed blood will purify them, and receive Jesus into your heart as Lord and Savior forever and receive the best gift life has to offer! It will change your life forever for good! For this, dear Daughter is your truest identity, a Beloved Daughter of God—*Gifted with Salvation!*

Prayer: Jesus, I confess that I am a sinner in need of a Savior. I give you my life and receive now your beautiful gift of salvation. Come into my heart as Lord and Savior now and forever! In Jesus' name, Amen.

RESTORED

"The Lord is my Shepherd, I shall not want. He makes me to lie down in green pastures; He leads me beside the still waters. He restores my soul; He leads me in the paths of righteousness for His name's sake."

PSALM 23:1-3 NKJV

Remember a time you were exhausted and then got a good night's sleep—how did you feel the next day? Rejuvenated? Restored? Brand new? Rest is an essential part of your basic need as a human being. You need it daily each night you sleep, and you also need it weekly as you dedicate one day to rest and enjoy the gift of Sabbath rest from the Lord. God planned it this way when He set the pattern at the beginning of the time, because He knew we would be busy doing all that He's placed on our heart to accomplish. Rest is key because it leads our body, mind and soul to restoration.

Beloved Daughter of God, your Heavenly Father has it all planned out perfectly. He knows the desires He placed in you when He formed you in your mother's womb. He has a beautiful path of righteousness He wants to lead you down, but you must surrender to His ways and joyfully embrace the way to get there. Your identity as His beloved Daughter is restored, but you must submit to His loving path of rest to enjoy it. Putting on the identity of Restored looks like daily times of rest, being still and quieting yourself before your loving Father to press into Him and His thoughts for you. When you are still in His presence, you quickly experience restoration as you hear once again what His loving thoughts are for you, know His good plans for your life, and become filled to overflowing with the joy He so abundantly has to offer. Rest in the world's eyes is sometimes looked down upon, as the world elevates busyness, accomplishments and working at all costs to achieve an end goal. While that can be great, busyness can quickly take you down a path of exhaustion, becoming overwhelmed and feeling stress. God can accomplish more in your time of rest leading to restoration in His miraculous ways than you can ever imagine. Get excited and embrace with confidence the path to restoration that Father God has for you awaiting each day as you rest. You will find yourself joyfully flourishing in this beautiful identity God gave you as His beloved Daughter, for it is your truest identity—*Restored!*

Prayer: Thank you God that your path is peace, your ways are wisdom, and your heart for me is love. Help me to enjoy your rest you are always offering so that I can fully walk in my truest identity, Restored! In Jesus' name, Amen.

HEALED BY HIS STRIPES

"But he was pierced for our transgressions, he was crushed for our iniquities;
the punishment that brought us peace was on him, and by his wounds we are healed."

Isaiah 53:5 NIV

In 2006, I went on a mission trip that changed my life forever. I surrendered all to Jesus and in return, He healed every sadness, hurt, and pain that life had thrown at me. The first night on the trip, the Lord led me to lay down a huge hurt from childhood and as hard as it was, I did it. The next night, at the church service I attended, the Lord showed up in a huge way and took away all sadness from my pain and turned it into joy!

Beloved Daughter of God, your loving Father has so many good things He wants to bless you with. Sometimes what holds us back is fear of giving up hurts and pains, or the unknown of what will happen if we forgive someone who hurt us. God is Jehovah Rapha, your Healer. It's not only His name, but His nature. He is the healer! Jesus died on the cross for your sin, sickness and death, and the Holy Spirit power that raised Jesus from the dead is alive in you!

When you place those things that are hurting inside of you at the foot of the cross, he hears you and he is at work to heal you. It may be immediate as you feel better, experience joy in the midst of suffering, hope in the midst of uncertainty, or faith in the face of a trial. It may also take time as God works in and through you to complete the good work that he has begun. Trust him to heal you in every way, because this is your truest identity as a Beloved Daughter of Christ—*Healed by His Stripes.*

Prayer: Jesus, your Word says that by your stripes I am healed. I need your healing today. Take away every doubt in my mind and cast down every lie that is contrary to this. I put my hope in you again today that nothing is impossible with you! I trust you and I receive my truest identity as Healed by Your Stripes! Amen.

IN THE PALM OF HIS HAND

"See, I have written your name on the palms of my hands."

Isaiah 49:16 NLT

When I was a child, we would go to Vacation Bible School every summer. It was a week long camp at church doing fun things, making crafts, singing songs, playing games, watching the stories of the Bible acted out and learning about Jesus. I remember singing the song, "He's got the whole world, in His hands…He's got the whole world, in His hands…." It would always amaze me when I would think about the gigantic world and everything that encompassed it, and God's Hand was bigger than that.

Beloved Daughter of God, as His child, you are in your Father's loving hand. His hand is one of protection, safety, comfort, provision, wisdom, guidance, love, peace, joy, and so much more. You are near and dear to your Father's loving embrace. You are never out of God's sight, as His eyes are ever upon you. You are never out of His reach either, as you are firmly in the strength of His embrace. Even though life may cause you to worry with its uncertainties and unexpected surprises, you are secure in the palm of God's hand. Take a moment to feel the weight of this truth. Say it aloud, "I am in the palm of your hand, Heavenly Father. I will walk in faith knowing whose care I am in." Remember that song? If His hand is big enough to hold the whole world in it, there is never anything too big for God to handle for you. Claim this truth and be firmly planted in this promise. For this is your truest identity as a beloved Daughter of God—*In the Palm of His Hand.*

Prayer: Thank you Lord that I am in the palm of your hand. Every time I look at my hands, I will envision myself in your hand because that is your promise and my identity! Thank you that you care for me and love me beyond measure! In Jesus' name, Amen.

ROYAL PRIESTHOOD

*"But you are a chosen people, a royal priesthood, a holy nation, God's special possession,
that you may declare the praises of him who called you out of darkness into his wonderful light."*

1 Peter 2:9 NIV

Every time I witness a new believer in Christ taking the step of faith in baptism, it sends chills up and down my body. Seeing someone being lowered into water symbolizing the old self being buried with Christ, and then bursting forth up into the air to represent resurrection with Christ in a new eternal life with him forever is glorious! In a single moment an invisible but very real supernatural transaction takes place during salvation when a son or daughter comes home and is once again united with Christ, adopted into His chosen people, a royal priesthood!

Beloved Daughter of God, have you given your life to Christ and died to the old self of sin and death? The free gift of salvation and forgiveness of sin is abundantly given by your Heavenly Father and available to anyone who will submit to the Lordship of Christ. Once this takes place, a new identity emerges from an orphan separated from God to perfect unity and His special possession as a royal priest of God! No longer will you walk in darkness and confusion, but into His glorious light, seeing from a new perspective and hearing clearly the wisdom, guidance and whispers of God Almighty through His Holy Spirit. No longer will you wake up hopeless, worried, or fearful, but as you understand your identity and position, praise upon praise will ever be upon your tongue! You have the hope of the world living powerfully within you! You have access to all joy, peace, and love, which conquers all. As you walk where the Lord leads, you will notice beautiful gifts generously awaiting you just because your good Father loves to lavish them upon you. What an empowering promise to hold on to and encourage others in! Go now and forge on boldly in your secure identity as a beloved Daughter of God—*A Royal Priesthood.*

Prayer: Heavenly Father, I humble myself before you the King of Kings and Lord of Lords grateful for this powerful identity as a royal priest for you. Teach me, lead me and guide me into stewarding well with love this beautiful gift to help every person you put in my path today and forever. In Jesus' name, Amen.

POWERFUL WITNESS OF CHRIST

"But you will receive power when the Holy Spirit comes on you;
and you will be my witnesses in Jerusalem, and in all Judea and Samaria,
and to the ends of the earth."

ACTS 1:8 NIV

Every summer, our family excitedly awaits our favorite trip of the year—the beach! As soon as we cross the bridge to Sullivan's Island, the beautiful historic lighthouse greets us, standing tall and strong! Captivating to the eye, it emerges from the trees so that anyone within a good distance can see it, but also purposed to see over all things as well. It is meant to be a light to wayward sailors and fisherman out at sea to find their way back, as well as a support to watch out for any encroaching danger to protect those in its territory. It stands tall as a beacon of light and witness to all creation to help anyone in need.

Beloved Daughter of God, what an amazing privilege Jesus gave you in the promise of Acts 1:8. When you placed your faith and trust in him as Lord and Savior, you received the fulfillment of this promise as the Holy Spirit came upon you. Just like the beautiful example of the physical lighthouse rising above the trees and ocean to give light to those around it, you too are a bright shining light for Christ as the hope of the world. The same Spirit that raised Christ from the dead is alive in you and when you align yourself with His leading and guidance, the great purposes of the Lord become reality. Your Heavenly Father has sent you to be His witness of His life changing love, peace, hope, strength, joy, forgiveness, and so much more. Keep your eyes focused on and ears sensitive to His whispers and be bold to speak, act and react wherever He leads and guides. Lives will be changed, hearts will be renewed, children restored to their eternal Father will be your continual experience as you allow this powerful love to flow through you to others. Get excited and take action, Beloved Daughter of God, for this is your truest identity—*A powerful witness of Christ*!

Prayer: Thank you Father for the privilege it is to be a witness of your amazing love, forgiveness and grace. Help me continually see with your perspective to connect others to you with this gift of love that has the power to change lives for all eternity! Amen.

NO LONGER A SLAVE TO SIN

*"For we know that our old self was crucified with him so that the body ruled
by sin might be done away with that we should no longer be slaves to sin because anyone
who has died has been set free from sin."*

ROMANS 6:6-7 NIV

The best dog we ever had was a yellow Labrador Retriever named Scout. I surprised my husband on his birthday with this adorable twelve week old lab puppy who had the best breathe and big clumsy feet. As Scout grew, so did his curiosity for chewing furniture and getting into trouble. Scout came from a champion bloodline of bird hunters, so when the time came my husband began training him into his God given purpose. Scout was very strong willed, so it took much patience and persistence to subdue the wild puppy nature into a calm well behaved talented bird hunter.

Beloved Daughter of God, when sin entered the world through Adam and Eve, so did the fallen sin nature that leads to death in every way. You were born with this nature that wants to make a self-god, leading to pride and destruction. But Jesus paid the price on the cross by crucifying the penalty once and for all so that you no longer have to be a slave to sin but are finally able to walk in your destiny and purpose freely as you choose daily to live by His Spirit and not your flesh.

You now have the choice to live free when you humble yourself under God and allow Him to train you in righteousness so that who He created you to become may be developed. You come from the champion bloodline of Jesus Christ and can walk in the overcoming life by following His leading. Take time daily to spend time listening to the Master Trainer for this is truly your heart's delight! For your truest identity as a beloved Daughter of God is free in Christ and No Longer a Slave to Sin!

*Prayer: Dear Jesus, thank you for freeing me from the power of sin and death.
I choose this day going forward to put myself under your loving training so that I may
become truly what you created me to be!*

SECURED FOR ETERNITY

"I am the gate; whoever enters through me will be saved.
They will come in and go out, and find pasture."

JOHN 10:9 NIV

Growing up in church, I gave my life to Christ at age twelve, but it wasn't until age twenty-six that I truly understood my relationship with Christ and the security that simple fact brings. Fear not freedom led my relationship with Jesus, striving to achieve a status of living as a "Christian." If I behaved well, I felt secure, and if I messed up, worry beat down the door of my mind challenging with the thought that I might lose my eternal security.

Beloved Daughter of God, let me destroy the powerful lie of the enemy that eternal security from God comes from what you do, or what you don't do. Nothing could be further from the truth. Jesus died on the cross to take your place and once you place your faith in him, you walk through the gate of powerful eternal security. In an instant you walk from darkness to light, and nothing you do can ever change that. The enemy wants to put a yoke of religion around your neck that chokes you until you fear security and walk through life on eggshells that you might mess up. Your identity is not in what you do, but in who you have chosen as Lord and Savior in your life. At salvation, an irrevocable transaction took place where you received the life Christ died to give you for the seed of death you were born with. The gates to the Kingdom of God opened and you became adopted as a Daughter of God once and forever. Even when you mess up (and you will) and your feelings want to shame you, reject those lies of insecurity and walk in the freedom and peace of your truest identity—*Beloved Daughter of God, Secured for Eternity.*

Prayer: Jesus thank you that you are the way, the truth, and the life. Thank you for the supernatural exchange you gave me when I placed my faith in you of eternal security. I receive the peace you have for me that my identity is not in what I do, but who I am, a beloved child of God.

LAVISHED WITH GIFTS

"Every good and perfect gift is from above, coming down from the Father of the heavenly lights, who does not change like shifting shadows."

JAMES 1:17 NIV

Have you ever had a surprise birthday party? A couple of years ago, my husband surprised me with a lavish celebration for my birthday. Family and friends awaited our arrival with love, joy and gifts to celebrate the occasion. A wonderful time was had by all with lots of laughter, time together, and a few gifts sprinkled in too!

Beloved Daughter of God, have you noticed all of the gifts your Heavenly Father surprises you with each day? If you woke up feeling joyful, that was Him. If you enjoyed some time with your family, He set that up. If you hit all the green lights on the way to work, God intervened on your behalf because He knew it would make you happy. How about that unexpected call from a friend that cheered you up? Yep, God prompted that friend to call you! Did you enjoy that delicious meal? God provided that just because He loves to lavish you with His good gifts. What about that strength you gained from the last trial you had to endure? And the testimony of faith that came from the testing that was so tough? All good things come from your Heavenly Father. Sometimes they come in fun surprises, and sometimes they are disguised amidst trials, but God has a perfect plan to express His unfathomable love in the form of beautiful gifts to you each and every day. But just as you might miss the beautiful fragrance of a rose if you didn't stop to smell it, you must pay attention in life to see all of the gifts that God gives you each day!

Every day can be like that surprise birthday if you look for the surprise gifts God has for you! You are lavished beyond measure with gifts from your good Father, for this is your truest identity as a beloved daughter of God!–Lavished with Gifts.

Prayer: Thank you Father that you lavish me with so many gifts each day! Help me to slow down, smell the roses and notice all of the gifts of love that you surprise me with! A grateful heart is a joyful heart, and I want eyes to see and ears to hear and a heart to respond!! Amen.

COMPLETE IN CHRIST

"For in Him all the fullness of Deity dwells in bodily form, and in Him you have been made complete, and He is the head over all rule and authority."

CoLOSSIANS 2:9-10 NASB

Growing up my favorite subject in school was always math. I loved the exactness of equations, and how they are black and white, wrong or right. When you solve a math problem for the first time, if a + b = c, then you know that to be the rule, or the truth, that you could prove to be correct every time.

Beloved Daughter of God, if you search the scriptures, you can look at God's promises as rules, or equations to be true every time. This is comforting to help you bypass all doubt and unbelief, because if God's Word is true (and we know it is!) then you can read every promise and accept it completely as truth for now and forever! In the promise Colossians 2:9-10, your identity as a beloved daughter of God is revealed. In Jesus Christ is the complete fullness of the Deity, or Godhead. That means all that God is, was in Jesus. And so, if you have given your life to Jesus as Lord and Savior, then you are in Jesus. If this is the case, then we have our math equation of a truth that you can stand on as your identity!! If (a) Jesus is over all + (b) you are in Jesus, then that = equals (c) You are complete in Christ! As you stand complete in Christ, then you also have the authority overall, so be confident in this faith and exercise it! If everything is under Christ's feet and you are in Christ, then it's under yours! You have everything you need in Christ for success and victory. It is Him working in and through you that produces the victory every time. Stay connected and firmly rooted in Him and He will continue to grow all of the wonderful and powerful gifts and good works He began in you at salvation! Stand tall and walk boldly and courageously no matter what beloved Daughter of God, because your truest identity is powerful, "Complete in Christ!"

Prayer: Dear Jesus, thank you that I am complete in you. Help me understand more and more this amazing identity you have given me as I keep my eyes focused on you and heart obedient to follow you. What an exciting adventure we have ahead together!

FORGIVEN

"If we confess our sins, he is faithful and just and will forgive us our sins and purify us from all unrighteousness."

1 John 1:9 NIV

Every time I travel, my favorite route is along the back roads of rural America. It is so delightful to see all the gorgeous farmlands as well as the quaintness of Small Town, USA. On one particular trip, as we traveled the fields were completely cleared, and only lush flat ground ripe for planting remained. All of the crops that were well past their prime and no good had been cleared to prepare for the next planting season. The soil, although completely bare, was a beautiful reminder of how this beautiful farmland resembled my soul the moment I received forgiveness for all of my sins past, present and future through the shed blood of Jesus Christ. Hallelujah!

Beloved Daughter of God, God's Word promises that once you realize you are a sinner and confess your sins to your Heavenly Father, He will forgive you. Yes, your once filthy sin stained condition gets completely purified with Jesus' precious blood and you appear as white as snow to God. They have all been cleared out, removed, and never again remembered. Just like that beautiful farmland, the soil of your heart becomes the perfect field to plant and reap an abundant harvest of God's purposes in your life. The Bible says that as far as the east is from the west is how far He has removed our sins! So, you too, when you look at your past, there should be absolutely no shame, no fear, no guilt for any mistakes or sins you have made, because you are completely forgiven. You can just look confidently towards the path the Lord is calling you each and every day and walk freely into it! You are set free from the chains of bondage those sins contained you in, because this yes this, Beloved Daughter of God is your truest identity—*Forgiven.*

Prayer: O praise the name of the Lord Most High, praise the name of Jesus! Jesus, thank you for washing me completely clean of all sin by your precious shed blood! I stand confidently forgiven and free of all guilt, shame and condemnation for I am forgiven once and for all eternity!

BROUGHT TO FULLNESS

"I pray that out of his glorious riches he may strengthen you with power through his Spirit in your inner being, so that Christ may dwell in your hearts through faith. And I pray that you, being rooted and established in love, may have power, together with all the Lord's holy people, to grasp how wide and long and high and deep is the love of Christ, and to know this love that surpasses knowledge—that you may be filled to the measure of all the fullness of God."

Ephesians 3:16-19 NIV

One of my favorite days of the year is Thanksgiving Day. It's our tradition every Thanksgiving Day for all of my family to gather together around midday at my parent's house, all bring a dish or two, and spend the day together playing games, telling stories, and enjoying lots of yummy food and wonderful fellowship! My husband and I forgo breakfast in anticipation of consuming our favorite foods and being wonderfully full! Every year is the same result…we are brought to complete fullness with a very happy heart from lots of love shared and extremely full stomach from indulging on scrumptious southern delicacies!

Beloved Daughter of God, your Heavenly Father wants to fill you up to overflowing with His love and goodness. Even more glorious than the best meal Thanksgiving could offer is God's love when you are filled by it! Your Father has greater riches than this world offers, love, joy, peace, hope, strength, power, courage, wisdom, and so much more. And the good news is that He wants you to have it abundantly!! As you come to know Him more and more, you will understand more how great His love is that conquers all. It is in the knowing your Lord and Savior that you know his beautiful love which fills you up in the best possible way! This fullness is everything amazing that God is: His presence, His love, His peace, His joy, His strength….and when you are full of Him, you don't want anything else!! Just by being His beloved daughter, you are welcomed each and every day to walk through the gate of Jesus to experience the beautiful gifts He's already prepared for you. For this identity is yours dear Daughter, so run hard after pursuing your good Father. Draw near to Him and He will so generously draw near to you. What an amazing trade He offers because He adores you! This is your truest identity as a Beloved Daughter of God—*Brought to Fullness.*

Prayer: How exciting Lord that you want to fill me up so full that I overflow with you! Teach me, help me, guide me in knowing you more and understanding your love for me! What a great identity and adventure awaits with you, my Lord and lover of my soul! In Jesus' name, Amen.

DEAR BELOVED DAUGHTER OF GOD,

With the close of this book and year-long journey with your loving Heavenly Father, a new door in life awaits you! As you now understand your truest identity in Christ, you can now walk boldly and courageously in what God has for you next! All throughout the Bible, when children of God truly knew who they were to their Father, they were unstoppable! Abraham took leaps of faith to move to a foreign land, waiting on the fulfillment of God's promises to make a mighty nation arise from his lineage. Moses fearlessly led all of the Israelites out of Egypt into the unknown to find God's Promised Land. Daniel courageously rejected the gods of His day risking his life in a hungry lion's den. David didn't back down to fight Goliath the Giant because he knew God was on his side. Joshua, called to spy out the long awaited Promised Land, didn't let the threat of defeat by giants who occupied the land scare him off. And Jesus, your Savior, who for the joy set before him (YOU!), endured the cross, scorning it's shame, and paid the complete price for your sins.

You now know the truth of who you are. With God, nothing is impossible. Be bold and claim it. Be courageous and walk it out. Be confident and take risks every day to accept all the future invitations God has for you! Life may throw some tough hills to climb, but you know that you can do all things through Jesus Christ who is alive and always by your side! Go now, and embrace this amazing identity God has bestowed upon you and enjoy doing life together with the One who is over all creation!

For God so loved the world that he gave his one and only Son, that whoever believes in him shall not perish but have eternal life." (John 3:16)